WRITING 4

AUG 15

D1706865

Expository
Writing

SADDLEBACK
EDUCATIONAL PUBLISHING

WRITING 4

Descriptive Writing

Expository Writing

Narrative Writing

Persuasive Writing

SADDLEBACK
EDUCATIONAL PUBLISHING
www.sdlback.com

© 2005, 2011, 2013 by Saddleback Educational Publishing

ISBN-13: 978-1-62250-025-3
ISBN-10: 1-62250-025-3
eBook: 978-1-61247-668-1

Printed in the United States of America

17 16 15 14 13   1 2 3 4 5

Contents

To the Student

How about it? Can *you* count on your writing skills to make your meaning clear?

Check yourself out by answering the following questions!

▶ Can you give other people easy-to-follow directions and explanations?

    EXAMPLES: **how to tape a TV show**
                      how a bill becomes law

▶ Can you describe something clearly enough to create a vivid image in the minds of your audience?

    EXAMPLES: **a dramatic thunderstorm**
                      a movie star's mansion

▶ Can you tell a story so well that your audience is fascinated from beginning to end?

    EXAMPLES: **the history of baseball**
                      the world's worst date

▶ Can you usually persuade others to accept your opinion or take some kind of action?

    EXAMPLES: **see a certain movie**
                      register to vote

Saddleback's WRITING 4 series will improve your written work—no matter what your purpose is for writing. If you make your best effort, the result will surprise you. You'll discover that putting words on paper isn't that much different from saying words out loud. The thought processes and grammatical structures are the same. Writing is just another form of expression; skill develops with practice!

Competent writers do better at school and at work. Keep that in mind as you work your way through these books. If you learn to write well, you're more likely to succeed in whatever you want to do!

Are you ready to go for it?
Follow me—I'm off and running!

Lesson
1
The Five Ws

The five Ws—*who, what, when, where,* and *why*—are important guidelines when you're writing to inform. Why? These key words remind you to include all the essential facts.

A. Read this bulletin board notice. Then answer the questions that follow.

 **ATTENTION PROM COMMITTEE!**

The prom committee will meet in Room 314 on Thursday, March 4, at 3:30 in the afternoon. All those interested in helping us get organized are welcome to attend. At the first meeting, we will decide on a theme for the dance. We will also establish subcommittees for decorations, entertainment, chaperones, refreshments, and election of the king and queen and their court. Meetings will be held every Thursday at the same time and place until the last week of May.

PLEASE DON'T SIGN UP IF YOU CAN'T SERVE ON THE COMMITTEE UNTIL PROM NIGHT!

1. *Who* is invited to come to the meeting?

   _____

2. *What* is on the agenda for the first meeting?

   _____

3. *When* is the first meeting going to be held?

   _____

4. *When* are subsequent meetings?

   _____

5. *Where* will the meetings be held?

   _____

6. *Why* are the meetings being held? (What is their purpose?)

   _____

B. Think about the five Ws as you read this newspaper story that might have appeared in the 1920s. Then answer the questions that follow.

EDERLE FIRST WOMAN TO SWIM CHANNEL

On August 6, nineteen-year-old Gertrude Ederle became the first woman to swim the English Channel. She completed her swim faster than any of the men who have done it over the last 51 years! The hardy New Yorker took 14 hours and 31 minutes to cross the Channel. The best previous time was 16 hours and 23 minutes by an Italian swimmer, Sebastian Tirabocchi. That event took place three years ago, in 1923.

Miss Ederle entered the surf at 7:09 A.M. at Cape Gris-Nez, France. A few spectators were there, but she scarcely acknowledged them as she walked into the water. After five hours of swimming, she was slowed somewhat when the wind increased. But her biggest delay came at the finish. In England, Miss Ederle was held up again by customs officials who insisted on questioning her before allowing her on shore.

1. *Who* are the two people mentioned by name in this story?

   _____

2. *What* newsworthy feat is being reported?

   _____

3. *When* did it happen?

   _____

4. *Where* did it happen?

   _____

5. This article does not tell *why* Gertrude Ederle swam the English Channel. Use your imagination to complete the following sentence:

   When asked why she wanted to be the first woman to swim the English

   Channel, Miss Ederle replied, "_____

   _____

   _____."

Lesson 2 Messages

Have you ever received a written message about a telephone call you missed? Did it give you enough information to return the call—or were some important facts left out? If you've ever received an incomplete message, you know how frustrating that can be.

A. Here's an example of a poorly written message about a telephone call. You have a two-part task. First, determine what information is missing. Second, rewrite the message to make it complete. (You will have to make up some details.)

Joan—A guy called you about Friday night. He said something about a dance. He wants you to call him back..

YOUR MESSAGE REWRITE

B. Practice taking a telephone message. Underline the important information as you read the following telephone conversation. Then write a message for Jake. Be sure to include all the information Jake needs to return the call.

YOU: Hello?

CALLER: Hello. Is Jake there?

YOU: No, he isn't. May I take a message?

CALLER: Yes. This is Barry Watson. I'm the manager of the new ice cream store on Birch Street. Jake applied for a part-time job here, and I want him to come in for an interview. Would you ask him to call me to arrange an appointment?

YOU: Of course, Mr. Watson. What would be a good time for him to call?

CALLER: Well, I'm here from noon to nine every day but Sunday. The phone number of the store is 555-3972.

YOU: Thank you, Mr. Watson. I'll give him the message.

CALLER: Thank you. Goodbye.

YOU: Bye.

YOUR MESSAGE TO JAKE

Lesson 3

Filling Out Forms

Businesses and organizations often require the use of informational forms. If you want to apply for a credit card, for example, you must fill out a special form. You will also fill out certain forms when you file tax reports, apply for a library card, or visit a doctor's office. What about buying insurance, applying for jobs, sending for rebates, or taking out loans? All these transactions require special forms.

A. Here's a form used by the United States Post Office. Suppose you're moving to a different house or apartment. Use the information below to fill out the form.

- You will move on the tenth of next month.

- Your new address will be 489 Erickson Avenue.

- You will live in the same city and have the same ZIP code that you have now.

OFFICIAL MAIL FORWARDING CHANGE OF ADDRESS FORM

U.S. Postal Service
CHANGE OF ADDRESS ORDER

Instructions: Complete Items 1 thru 10. You must SIGN Item 9. Please PRINT all other items including address on face of card.

OFFICIAL USE ONLY

Zone/Route ID No.

1. Change of Address for: (See instruction #1 above)
   ☐ Individual   ☐ Entire Family   ☐ Business

2. Start Date: Month Day Year

Date Entered on Form 3982
M M D D Y Y

3. Is This Move Temporary? (Check one)
   ☐ No   ☐ Yes, Fill in ▶

4. If TEMPORARY move, print date to discontinue forwarding: Month Day Year

Expiration Date
M M D D Y Y

5. Print Last Name (include Jr., Sr., etc.) or Name of Business (If more than one, use separate form for each).

Clerk/Carrier Endorsement

6. Print First Name (or Initial) and Middle Name (or Initial). Leave blank if for a business.

7a. For Puerto Rico Only: If OLD mailing address is in Puerto Rico, print urbanization name, if appropriate.

7b. Print OLD mailing address: House/Building Number and Street Name (include St., Ave., Rd., Ct., etc.).

Apt./Suite No.   or   PO Box No.   or ☐RR/ ☐HCR (Check one)   RR/HCR Box No.

City   State   ZIP Code   ZIP+4

8a. For Puerto Rico Only: If NEW mailing address is in Puerto Rico, print urbanization name, if appropriate.

8b. Print NEW mailing address: House/Building Number and Street Name (include St., Ave., Rd., Ct., etc.).

Apt./Suite No.   or   ☐ PO Box No. / ☐ PMB No. (Check one)   or ☐RR/ ☐HCR   ☐PMB No./☐RR/HCR Box No.

City   State   ZIP Code   ZIP+4

9. Sign and Print Name (see conditions on reverse)
   Sign: _____
   Print:

10. Date Signed: Month Day Year

OFFICIAL USE ONLY
Verification Endorsement

PS FORM 3575, September 2001   See http://www.usps.com/moversnet for more information.   0091

B. Many employers require you to keep track of your working hours on a time card. Use the information below to complete the time card.

- For the date, use last week.

- Your usual working hours are 8:00 A.M. to 5:00 P.M. You get paid for eight hours of work (regular pay) and take a one-hour lunch (unpaid). In column 2, do *not* include your lunch hour. You get paid time-and-a-half for overtime, which is anything over eight hours a day.

- Monday was a holiday. It is paid as if it were a regular day.

- On Tuesday, you worked a regular day.

- Wednesday was a busy day. You worked from 8:00 A.M. to 7:00 P.M. You took a 30-minute lunch break.

- On Thursday, you worked a regular day.

- On Friday, you worked from 8:00 A.M. to 5:00 P.M. You went to the doctor from 2:00 P.M. to 3:30 P.M. This time is covered by sick pay.

TIME CARD

Week of: _____

Employee: _____

DAY OF WEEK	TOTAL HOURS WORKED	REGULAR PAY	SICK PAY	VACATION PAY	OVERTIME
MON.					
TUES.					
WED.					
THURS.					
FRI.					

Prewriting: Gathering Resource Information

Suppose you are assigned to write an essay based on research. The quality and quantity of the information you gather is important. What questions about your subject are you going to investigate? Begin by listing these questions. Then consult the sources that are most likely to be helpful in answering your questions.

A. What topic will you select for your essay? You might want to write about politics, history, biology, culture, or ethics. Alternatively, you may write about anything else that interests you.

Write your essay topic here: _____

Now write five questions about your topic. After each question, write the source you would consult to get the answer. These sources might be encyclopedias, atlases, almanacs, newspapers, magazines, or documentaries. They might also include electronic databases on CD-ROMs or on the Internet, personal interviews of experts, biographies, or primary sources such as journals and diaries.

1. _____

_____

_____

2. _____

_____

_____

3. _____

_____

_____

4. _____

_____

_____

5. _____

_____

_____

B. Here are the questions one student planned to answer about the topic, *Frank Lloyd Wright: Master Architect*. After each question, write a source that would likely have the answer.

GUGGENHEIM MUSEUM
NEW YORK, NY
DESIGNED BY
Frank Lloyd Wright

1. When did Frank Lloyd Wright live? Who were his parents, and where was he born?

   _____

   _____

2. Suppose I want to visit Wright's most famous building, Fallingwater, near Mill Run, Pennsylvania. How far would I have to travel to see it?

   _____

3. Why did Wright say that he chose architecture as his career?

   _____

4. What is the price of admission to New York City's Guggenheim Museum, a building designed by Wright?

   _____

5. Suppose I visited Taliesin West, the winter home of the Frank Lloyd Wright School of Architecture in Scottsdale, Arizona. What recreational and cultural activities would be available to me in that area?

   _____

6. What did some of Wright's clients think of the buildings the gifted architect designed for them?

   _____

7. What kind of childhood did Frank Lloyd Wright have?

   _____

8. Frank Lloyd Wright was married three times, yet he is buried next to a woman he never married. What's the story behind that?

   _____

Lesson 4

Résumé and Cover Letter

A résumé is a written statement of your own background. Serving as an introduction, it lists personal information such as your address and phone number. It also outlines your education and lists your work experience, duties, and skills. The usual purpose of a résumé is to impress a future employer enough to give you a job interview.

An effective résumé isn't too long or wordy. Your goal is to supply pertinent information as clearly and concisely as possible.

A. Read these groups of sentences or phrases that might appear on a résumé. Put a check mark (✓) by the one you think is *most* likely to get you an interview. (Hint: Look for specific details.) Then explain why you chose that sentence.

1. _____ I was in charge of sandwiches.
   _____ I made many sandwiches each day.
   _____ Prepared 15 sandwiches per hour.

   _____

2. _____ My duties included filing correspondence.
   _____ Filed correspondence for three attorneys.
   _____ I was the only file clerk in a busy law office.

   _____

3. _____ Greeted clients, answered the phone, and made appointments.
   _____ Was the receptionist at Johanssens's Hair Salon.
   _____ Worked at Johanssens's Hair Salon.

   _____

4. _____ I decided to open a bike-repair shop.
   _____ Owned and operated a busy bike-repair shop for two years.
   _____ Was the owner of a bike-repair shop.

   _____

5. _____ Among other duties, closing the shop at night was a job assigned to me.
   _____ I was the one who had to close the shop at night.
   _____ Closed the shop and secured the building at the end of each workday.

   _____

When you send a résumé to a potential employer, you need to send a cover letter as well. The best cover letters are short and to the point. Here is an example of an appropriate cover letter.

1132 Erickson Avenue
Fountain Valley, CA 92728
May 6, 2004

Jasmine E. Martinez, Manager
Martinez Framing Shop
483 Elmhurst Drive
Fountain Valley, CA 92728

Dear Ms. Martinez:

Having seen your ad for an assistant in Saturday's newspaper, I would like to apply for the job.

I will be graduating from high school in June and will then be available for full-time work. I am an avid amateur photographer, and I have some experience framing my own photographs for various exhibits and contests. I am eager to learn more about framing photographs, posters, and fine art.

My résumé is enclosed.

Sincerely,

Janet Summers

Janet Summers

B. Using the example as a model, write a cover letter of your own on a separate piece of paper. Address it to the Human Resources Department, Capital City Insurance Company, 1837 C Street, Sacramento, CA 95813. You're answering an ad for a receptionist. Include any additional information you think is important.

Lesson 5

Office Memo, E-Mail

A *memo* is a short note meant to communicate a message within an office or within a company. Correct spelling and grammar are just as important in a memo as they are in more formal business writing. When you write a memo, make your point by using simple words and short, complete sentences. Stick to the facts that matter, using a topic sentence, supporting sentences, and a closing.

A. Imagine that you have just been promoted. You are now the manager of a sandwich shop. You are writing a memo to all the employees, letting them know you are open to ideas for improvement. You want these ideas brought to you either before or after the employees' shifts. Alternatively, they may call you at home between certain hours.

To organize your ideas, complete the outline below. Then write the memo on the shop's memo form.

OUTLINE

TOPIC SENTENCE: _____

SUPPORTING SENTENCES: _____

_____

CLOSING SENTENCE: _____

MEMO

Date: _____

To: _____

From: _____

Regarding: _____

Message: _____

_____

_____

_____

_____

_____

E-mail, like an office memo, is less formal than a regular business letter. Business e-mail, however, is more formal than the casual e-mail you exchange with your friends. Follow these rules for business e-mail:

- Do not use playful images such as smiley faces.

- Do not use abbreviations such as "How R U?"

- If possible, keep your message short enough to fit on the screen. It's best if your reader does not have to scroll down to read it.

- Use standard spelling and grammar.

B. Imagine that you work for a florist. A customer has ordered a flower arrangement to be delivered to an address in another state. The customer wants pink roses, white orchids, yellow daffodils, and purple irises. She does not want to spend more than $90.00. You will have the order filled by a friend of yours who has a floral business in that state.

Write an e-mail to your friend describing the arrangement and saying where to deliver it. (You'll have to make up an address.) Discuss payment arrangements as well. (Tell your friend to send an invoice and you'll send a check, minus your 20 percent commission.)

Lesson 6

How-To Directions

"How-to" directions explain the steps involved in completing a process from start to finish. Effective step-by-step directions are written in the order in which the steps should be carried out. A good way to organize such directions is to use a list marked by bullets (•), numbers, or letters.

A. Rewrite the steps below in chronological order.

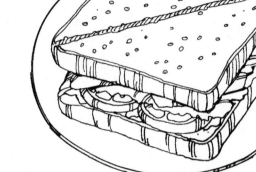

1. Arrange lettuce and tomato on the other slice of bread.

2. Arrange turkey slices and cheese on one slice of bread.

3. Assemble these supplies on the counter: loaf of bread, sliced turkey, sliced cheese, lettuce leaves, sliced tomato, mayonnaise.

4. Place the bread slices side by side on a plate.

5. Put a thin layer of mayonnaise on each slice of bread.

6. Slice sandwich in halves or quarters.

7. Put the two halves of the sandwich together.

8. Remove two slices of bread from the package.

1. _____

2. _____

3. _____

4. _____

5. _____

6. _____

7. _____

8. _____

B. Write step-by-step directions for any one of the following processes (or any topic of your own choosing). Break the job into at least nine steps.

- how to cook your favorite recipe
- how to play your favorite game
- how to wrap a birthday present
- how to make an ice cream sundae
- how to paint a room
- how to set a table
- how to wash a car
- how to give a dog a pill

How to _____

1. _____
   _____

2. _____
   _____

3. _____
   _____

4. _____
   _____

5. _____
   _____

6. _____
   _____

7. _____
   _____

8. _____
   _____

9. _____

Sentences: Adding Details

Details make your writing clearer and more interesting. Descriptive adjectives and adverbs are useful details. You can also use phrases and clauses that give more information about your topic. Compare the example sentences to get an idea of the difference a few details can make.

> **EXAMPLE SENTENCES**
> - Maria has a dog.
> - My friend Maria has a golden retriever whose fur is the same beautiful color as her own hair.

A. Try your hand at adding details to make these boring sentences more interesting.

1. Dan got a haircut today.

   _____

2. Maureen ordered a sandwich for lunch.

   _____

3. Jack's grandfather gave him a car.

   _____

4. Barbara wore an interesting outfit to the club.

   _____

5. Roger inherited a desk from his aunt.

   _____

6. Janice prepared dessert for her family.

   _____

7. Wesley is taking karate lessons.

   _____

8. Sylvia painted her bedroom.

   _____

9. Jacob gave a speech.

   _____

10. Antoinette makes necklaces.

    _____

B. Now write an interesting, detailed paragraph about any one of the following topics: a sports event, a holiday celebration, a dramatic performance, a hospital visit, a flower garden, or a busy restaurant. Before you begin, fill in the graphic organizer below. List sensory details that would make your paragraph more interesting.

How does it LOOK?	How does it SOUND?	How does it SMELL?	How does it TASTE?	How does it FEEL?

Lesson 7

First-Aid Instructions

First-aid instructions must be clear, easy to understand, and listed in step-by-step order. Remember that the reader must be able to quickly see what to do and what not to do! Often, first-aid instructions are presented in a bulleted or numbered list. Sometimes, they are also accompanied by illustrations. Here is an example:

FIRST AID FOR A CHOKING VICTIM, AGE 12 MONTHS TO ADULT

Symptoms: Person has difficulty speaking, coughing, or breathing

If you suspect that the airway is blocked by a foreign body, perform the Heimlich maneuver:

1. Stand behind the victim and wrap your hands around his or her waist.

2. Make a fist with one hand. Place the thumb side of your fist against the victim's abdomen halfway between the navel and the end of the breastbone.

3. Grab your fist with your other hand. Press the fist onto the abdomen with a quick upward and inward thrust (see illustration).

4. Repeat the Heimlich maneuver up to five times. Check to see if object has been coughed up.

5. Continue the Heimlich maneuver in cycles of five abdominal thrusts until one of the following occurs:

   a. The obstruction is expelled from the mouth.

   b. The person loses consciousness.

   c. Medical help arrives.

Following the example on page 22, write first-aid instructions for treating minor cuts and wounds. Before you begin, read the following paragraphs. Use whatever information you think is necessary. You may use a bulleted list, a numbered list, or a lettered list. If you wish, add an illustration.

The most important thing to remember in treating minor wounds is to prevent infection. Never put your mouth over a wound, breathe directly onto a wound, or touch the wound with your bare hands. Any of these actions would spread bacteria that could infect the wound.

The wound and surrounding skin must be cleaned immediately. Use soap and warm water, wiping away from the wound. In the case of active bleeding, hold a clean pad (clean handkerchief or clean cloth) firmly over the wound until the bleeding stops. If bleeding continues, add pads. Do not remove first pad. Do not use any fluffy material as a pad.

To help stop the bleeding, bandage the wound tightly with a triangular or rolled bandage. If bleeding does not stop, seek expert medical help immediately.

ILLUSTRATION

Lesson 8

Transportation Directions

Suppose someone asks you for directions from one place to another. You can be sure that he or she wants those directions to be as simple as possible. Information about landmarks such as "the big oak tree" is not very helpful. The most useful information is clear, direct, and specific. Suppose you asked someone for directions. Which of these two sentences would you rather hear? Put a check mark (✓) in the box next to the better answer.

❑ When you get to the corner of Fifth and Maple, turn left and go four blocks to Quince.

❑ When you see the house with the English garden in front, you're almost there.

No doubt you'd prefer the first. It gives exact information that is easy to verify.

A. Study this map. Then read the directions that follow. Use your finger to trace the route on the map.

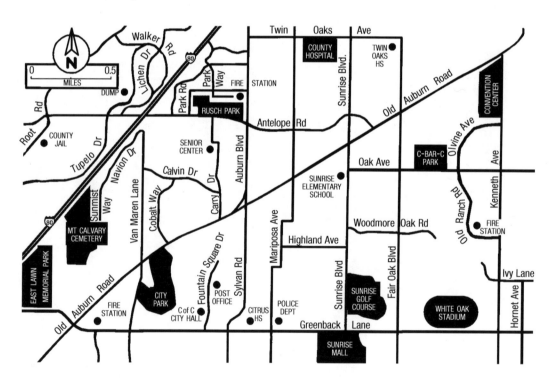

To get from Sunrise Mall to Rusch Park:

• Go west on Greenback Lane until you get to Sylvan Road.

• Turn right and go about 1½ miles to Antelope Road. (Notice that Sylvan Road becomes Auburn Boulevard when you cross Old Auburn Road.)

• Keep going straight until you get to Antelope Road.

• You'll see Rusch Park at the northwest corner of Antelope Road and Auburn Boulevard.

B. Using the map on page 24, write directions from City Hall to Mt. Calvary Cemetery.

_____

_____

_____

_____

_____

_____

_____

C. Now, choose any two places on the map that are least two miles apart. Write directions on how to get from one to the other.

_____

_____

_____

_____

_____

_____

_____

_____

Lesson 9

Product Warning Label

Have you noticed that many products have warning labels? This information explains the dangers of misusing the product and suggests cautions for safe use. Here is an example from a bottle of nail polish:

CAUTION

- Flammable. Keep away from heat and flame. Keep out of the reach of children. Harmful if taken internally.

- In case of accidental ingestion, contact the local Poison Control Center and seek emergency medical treatment.

- May be harmful to clothing, furnishings, and plastic.

A. Write your own product warning label for a container of medicine. Be thorough! Explain the purpose of the medicine, directions for use, and warnings about misuse. Invent any details that seem reasonable to you.

B. Now imagine that you have designed a new toy for children. First, draw a picture of your toy and describe it.

C. Now write the product warning label for your new toy. Remember to include warnings about the packaging itself.

Grammar: Pronoun-Antecedent Agreement

Remember that each pronoun in your writing must agree with its in number and gender. (An antecedent is the noun or nouns to which the pronoun refers.) Here are a few examples:

<u>Sandra</u> carried a bright pink umbrella as <u>she</u> took a stroll in the park.

<u>Bobby and Ted</u> walked through puddles, getting <u>their</u> boots and socks all wet.

A word's shows whether it is masculine, feminine, or neuter.

A. Draw an arrow from the underlined pronoun to its antecedent. Then, if the sentence shows pronoun-antecedent agreement, write "correct" on the line. If not, rewrite the sentence correctly. The first one has been done for you.

1. When the museum opened, crowds of people swarmed through <u>their</u> doors.

    When the museum opened, crowds of people swarmed through its doors.

2. A young woman sat before an easel, <u>her</u> eyes fixed on the canvas.

    _____

3. A large crowd gathered around the woman as <u>he</u> painted.

    _____

4. Ms. Stevens has a hobby that <u>she</u> thoroughly enjoys.

    _____

5. She chooses paintings she likes and makes copies of <u>it</u>.

    _____

6. Artists who copy the masters improve <u>your</u> own techniques.

    _____

7. Many artists have made copies of great masterpieces, selling <u>it</u> to clients.

    _____

8. Not everyone wants to sell the copies <u>they</u> have made.

    _____

9. Sally copies great paintings because she cannot afford to buy <u>it</u>.

    _____

10. To prevent forgeries, a copy cannot be the same size as the original <u>they</u> represent.

    _____

B. Rewrite this paragraph, correcting the pronoun-antecedent errors. If necessary, change the verb to agree in number with the pronoun or its antecedent. When you make this correction, you may have to change other words as well.

Since the day they opened in November 1793, the Louvre has allowed artists to copy the masterpieces it owns. In fact, it encourages you to come in and paint copies. French citizens fill out a simple form stating the date he wishes to begin and the painting he wishes to copy. Non-French artists must also attach a copy of their passport and a recommendation from your embassy. The Louvre has an official stamp that she affixes to both sides of each copy. Copies of masterpieces must be one-fifth smaller or larger than originals, and it must also be inspected before leaving the museum.

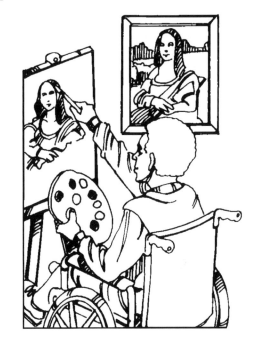

_____

_____

_____

_____

_____

_____

_____

_____

_____

_____

_____

Lesson 10 Product Labels

Food product labels often list more than just the contents and nutritional facts. They might give heating directions, special recipes, or interesting information about the product. Here is part of a product label for an imaginary brand of baked beans:

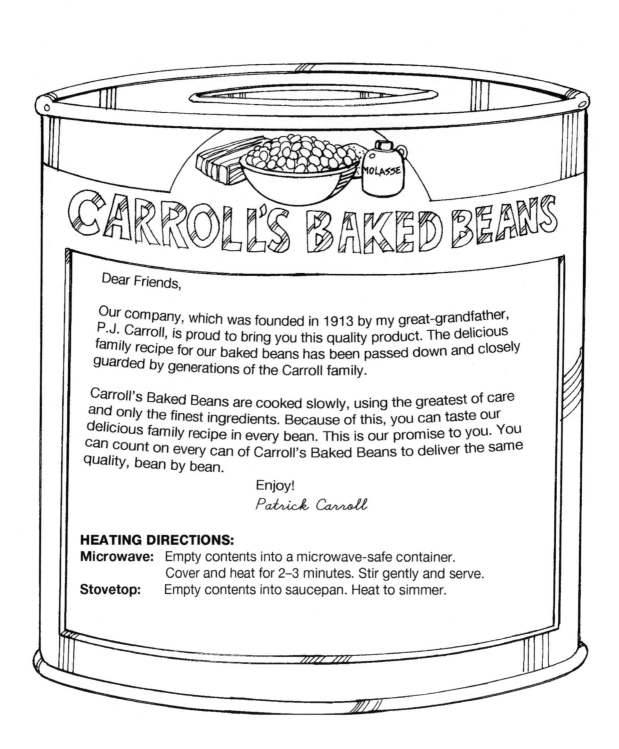

CARROLL'S BAKED BEANS

Dear Friends,

Our company, which was founded in 1913 by my great-grandfather, P.J. Carroll, is proud to bring you this quality product. The delicious family recipe for our baked beans has been passed down and closely guarded by generations of the Carroll family.

Carroll's Baked Beans are cooked slowly, using the greatest of care and only the finest ingredients. Because of this, you can taste our delicious family recipe in every bean. This is our promise to you. You can count on every can of Carroll's Baked Beans to deliver the same quality, bean by bean.

Enjoy!

Patrick Carroll

HEATING DIRECTIONS:
Microwave: Empty contents into a microwave-safe container. Cover and heat for 2–3 minutes. Stir gently and serve.
Stovetop: Empty contents into saucepan. Heat to simmer.

Imagine that it is your job to write a product label for a packaged food. Using the example on page 30 as a model, write a label for that food. Include cooking directions and suggestions for serving. In addition, write a brief letter to the consumer. In your letter, try to convince your customer that your product is truly special. You might also wish to include nutrition facts, a list of ingredients, and a company address.

(PRODUCT NAME)

(LETTER TO THE CONSUMER)

(COOKING DIRECTIONS, SERVING SUGGESTIONS, NUTRITIONAL FACTS, INGREDIENTS, COMPANY ADDRESS)

Lesson 11

Writing to Compare and Contrast

When writing to compare, you show how two things are alike and/or different. When writing to contrast, you focus only on the differences between two things.

A. Read the following list of pairs. For each pair, consider whether you would rather discuss how the items are similar (compare), how they are similar and different (compare), or only how they are different (contrast). Explain why you think so. As an example, the first one has been done for you.

1. *a vegetarian diet / a vegan diet*
   Contrast. Because these two diets are very similar, presenting the one major difference (i.e., a vegetarian diet allows dairy and eggs) would be the most concise way to differentiate the diets.

2. *swimming in a river / swimming in a pool*
   _____
   _____
   _____

3. *your two favorite books of fiction*
   _____
   _____
   _____

4. *attend college / attend trade school*
   _____
   _____
   _____

5. *living in an apartment / living in a house*
   _____
   _____
   _____

6. *being an only child / being one of several children*
   _____
   _____
   _____

7. *shopping online / shopping in a store*
   _____
   _____
   _____

B. Now choose three sets of pairs from page 32. For each one, write two supporting sentences that could be used in an essay of comparison, comparison and contrast, or contrast about that topic. Use the example as a guide.

Example: *Gen. Robert E. Lee /*
Gen. Ulysses S. Grant

1. *Lee was tall, handsome, and always wore an impressive uniform with a sword belted at his waist.*

2. *Grant, short and rough-looking, wore a rumpled blue private's coat with his general's stars tacked to the shoulders. He carried no sword.*

Topic 1: _____

1. _____
   _____
2. _____
   _____

Topic 2: _____

1. _____
   _____
2. _____
   _____

Topic 3: _____

1. _____
   _____
2. _____
   _____

Lesson 12

Announcements and Invitations

Suppose you were about to graduate from high school or college. You'd be eager to announce the good news to family and friends, wouldn't you? Graduations, weddings, births, birthdays, anniversaries—all these events prompt us to send out announcements and invitations.

Study this example of a wedding invitation:

Carla and Stephen Applewood
cordially invite you to the wedding of their daughter

Sharon Marie

to William Grandfield, son of Ed and Rita Grandfield

The ceremony will take place on
Saturday, April 17, 2004, at 3:00 P.M.
at the First Congregational Church,
4832 Oak Street, Roseville.
A reception will immediately follow.
R.S.V.P. by March 31.

A. Write your own announcement or invitation on the lines below. Be sure to include important details such as who, what, when, where, and why.

_____

_____

_____

_____

_____

_____

_____

_____

Sometimes, of course, sad news, such as someone's death, must be announced. This type of announcement is called an *obituary*. Obituaries usually appear in newspapers and magazines. They usually include highlights of the person's life, including dates of birth and death. They may also name surviving family members, and tell how the person will be remembered.

B. Write two obituary announcements on the lines below. Your subjects may be real people (former presidents, inventors, musicians, friends, or relatives) or fictional characters (Scrooge, Paul Bunyan, Homer Simpson). Use actual dates and biographical facts if you're writing about real people who have died. Make up appropriate details about fictional characters.

OBITUARIES

1.

2.

Mechanics: Proofreading

Error-free work makes a great impression. Take the time to check your manuscript for careless mistakes! Proofreading is one of the last steps in the writing process. When you proofread, you mark errors in your work so you can correct them in your final draft. Study the standard editing marks in the chart below.

EDITOR'S MARK	MEANING	EXAMPLE
ℓ	delete	The the fish swam away.
≡	capitalize	four students got perfect scores.
/	use lowercase	The Ballerina wore a blue tutu.
∧	insert a word	Doris has a cup of coffee.
RO	run-on sentence	The bell rang a child was at the door.
frag.	sentence fragment	Throughout the entire year.
sp	spelling error	Barbara was embarassed.
�U	transpose letters or words	Marna wrote stories four for the magazine.
⊙	add a period	Jack gave Georgia a bracelet ⊙
∧,	add a comma	We grow oranges, lemons, and peaches.
∨'	add an apostrophe	Saras favorite color is pink.
ⱽ⁶⁶ ⱽ⁹⁹	add quotation marks	Erin replied, I'd love to!
¶	begin a new paragraph	"Welcome to our home!" said Marie. "Thanks for inviting us," said Carl.
#	make a space	Do you like chocolate milk?
⌣	close a space	Where's the flash light?

Use the proofreading marks on page 36 to indicate necessary changes in the items below. Then write the sentences correctly on the lines.

1. The Vaganova ballet academy is a dance school in St. Petersburg.

_____

_____

2. This russian ballet school was founded in 1738

_____

3. The school is is named after Agrippini vaganova, one of its Teachers.

_____

_____

4. Potential students have must a medical examin ation before enrolling.

_____

_____

5. Classesand practice each day, six days a weak, for eight years.

_____

_____

6. For every student admitted, nine are turned away about 60 are admitted each year.

_____

_____

7. For practice, students may ware tights leotards and shorts.

_____

_____

8. Wouldnt you like to join american ballet company? Emma asked. I'd prefer to study someplace in europe Mikhail replied

_____

_____

Lesson 13   Planning for an Interview

Before you can be hired for a job, you will be interviewed. A good way to prepare for an interview is to make a list of questions you are likely to be asked. Then, prepare a good answer for each question.

A. Here are some questions a job interviewer might ask. Write good answers to the questions. Use complete sentences as you try to project an image of confidence and strength.

1. Why do you want to work here?

   _____

   _____

2. Do you have experience in this kind of work? What have you done?

   _____

   _____

3. How will you get to work every day?

   _____

   _____

4. What are your strengths as an employee?

   _____

   _____

5. What are your weaknesses as an employee?

   _____

   _____

6. Why should we hire you instead of someone else?

   _____

   _____

7. Why did you leave your other jobs?

   _____

   _____

Interviews are not always about jobs. You might conduct an interview to get information from an expert, an eyewitness, or a celebrity. Perhaps you want to interview a grandparent about family history. Or maybe you're after first-hand information about how it felt to make a winning touchdown.

B. Think of someone you'd like to interview. Who is it?

_____

Why do you want to interview this person?

_____

Think about the things your readers would want to know. Finally, write a list of questions you would ask. Then, write the answer you think that person might give. Use your imagination!

1. QUESTION: _____

   ANSWER: _____

   _____

2. QUESTION: _____

   ANSWER: _____

   _____

3. QUESTION: _____

   ANSWER: _____

   _____

4. QUESTION: _____

   ANSWER: _____

   _____

5. QUESTION: _____

   ANSWER: _____

   _____

Lesson
14   Taking Notes

Good note-taking skills are important in everyday situations as well as in school. When you take notes, be sure to include information about *who, what, when, where, why,* and *how*. Since notes are for your own personal use, you don't have to use complete sentences. Use phrases that will help you remember the information you will need later.

A. Explain how notes can help in each of the following situations. Write the specific information each person should include in his or her notes.

1. Myra needs to go to the main county library. She hasn't been there before.

   _____

   _____

2. Jon is the only one at home. Someone calls and wants to leave an important message for Jon's father.

   _____

   _____

3. David is comparing computer prices. As he calls and visits many stores, he is learning about many different brands, features, prices, and options.

   _____

   _____

4. Alicia needs to get to her new job. She will have to take three different buses to get there.

   _____

   _____

5. Jerome is watching TV. He sees a story about a skateboarding contest in town. He wants to go and see it.

   _____

   _____

6. Pat is listening to a lecture in his history class. It's about the Vietnam War. The test will be in a week.

   _____

   _____

B. Here are one person's notes for a report on the koala. Read them carefully. Then, using the notes, write a detailed paragraph about the animal. Use complete sentences.

Koala. Marsupial mammal from coastal eastern Australia. 21-33 inches long.

Body: pale gray or yellowish. No tail. Face: broad. Nose: big, round, leathery. Eyes: small, yellow. Ears: fluffy. Feet: strong-clawed. Opposable digits on hands and feet. Diet: eucalyptus leaves, about 3 pounds a day.

• Has one baby at a time. Baby stays in pouch for up to 7 months. Clings to mother's back until 12 months old.

Life expectancy: 20 years.

The Koala

_____

_____

_____

_____

_____

_____

_____

_____

_____

_____

_____

_____

Lesson 15

Short-Answer Test Questions

Short-answer tests usually require no more than two or three sentences to answer each question. When you take a short-answer test, make your answers direct and to the point. Write in complete sentences and stay focused: Don't include any information that was not specifically requested.

Scan each of the five questions and sample answers in this lesson. Then describe what's wrong with each sample answer.

Now, using the information provided, write a *better* answer for each question.

1. **What causes earthquakes?**

   Sample answer: The severity of an earthquake can be measured by an instrument called a *seismograph*. Sensitive seismographs can detect strong earthquakes from any part of the world. Forces deep within the earth continually affect the earth's surface. The energy from these forces is stored within the rocks. When this energy is released suddenly, an earthquake occurs.

   _____

   _____

   _____

   _____

   _____

2. **Name two important non-native explorers of North America. Tell where they came from, what they did, and when they did it.**

   Sample answer: Ponce de León came from Spain and explored Florida in 1513. This was about 21 years after Christopher Columbus discovered America. Another famous explorer was Hernando Cortés, a Spanish adventurer who conquered Mexico in 1519–1521. His name is also spelled Cortez. I think that what Cortés did to the Aztecs was just terrible.

   _____

   _____

   _____

   _____

   _____

3. **What is a "hung jury," and how does it affect a trial?**

Sample answer: A jury that is unable to reach a verdict of guilty or not guilty is called a "hung jury." When this happens, the result is a mistrial. One stubborn juror caused a hung jury in a recent murder trial in our city. If prosecutors want to bring the case to trial again, they must start over.

_____

_____

_____

_____

4. **What is the popular name for the Mesozoic Era, and what period of time did this era cover?**

Sample answer: The Mesozoic Era is more popularly known as the Age of Reptiles. This era began 245 million years ago and lasted for 180 million years. The word "Mesozoic" comes from the Greek word _mesos_ (middle) and _zoön_ (animal). No humans were alive during this time.

_____

_____

_____

_____

5. **What is the Taj Mahal? Who built it, and when?**

Sample answer: We visited the Taj Mahal on our trip to India last year, and it was the highlight of our vacation. The Taj Mahal is a marble mausoleum in India. It was built in the seventeenth century by a king for his wife. This structure usually appears on lists of the most beautiful buildings in the world.

_____

_____

_____

_____

Vocabulary: Precise Word Choice

Have you ever noticed that some words and phrases are overused? If someone tells you that he had a "nice time" at a party, what does he mean? If someone else says that the party was "good," what does she mean? Your communication will be much more effective if you use words that have precise meanings.

A. Replace each underlined word with a more precise synonym. Refer to a dictionary or a thesaurus if you need to. Be careful with connotations (the *suggested* meanings of words).

1. Rebecca bought a very (cute) _____ dress for the dance.

2. Marlene was such a (good) _____ Web site designer that she got a raise after just six months.

3. No one wants to babysit there because those children are so (bad) _____.

4. George (said) _____ to the operator that his neighbor's house was on fire.

5. The last movie Robert saw was especially (scary) _____.

6. After their long separation, Rosa was (happy) _____ to see her old friend again.

7. When Stanley's parents saw his poor report card, they were very (sad) _____.

8. The (pretty) _____ sunset was a fitting end to a perfect day.

9. Sara and Erin (went) _____ to the neighbors' house to report the emergency.

10. The gardener did a (nice) _____ job in the backyard.

11. The ice cream was so (good) _____ that Carla had a second serving.

12. The defendant (said) _____ that he was not guilty.

Can you imagine how boring sports news would be if the reporters didn't vary the language a bit? What if sports writers used only the words *lost* and *won* to describe the results of a game? The excitement of the story would be lost. When writers discuss sports, they make it interesting by using many different synonyms for *lost* and *won*.

B. For each score below, write a news headline that would describe the outcome of the game. Each time, use a different synonym for *lost* or *won*. Refer to a thesaurus for help. Make sure your synonym is appropriate. That is, do not use a word like *overwhelmed* for a score of 24 to 23.

1. Center High 144, East High 88

_____

2. Washington 12, Jefferson 10

_____

3. Sierra 48, Alemany 6

_____

4. San Mateo 12, Burlingame 4

_____

5. Galileo 24, Columbus 23

_____

6. Springfield 8, Woodside 2

_____

7. Taylor 143, Polk 70

_____

8. Ross 43, Jamestown 38

_____

Lesson 16

Thesis Statements for Essay Questions

In a composition, the *thesis statement* is a statement of purpose. It usually appears in the first paragraph. A good thesis statement for an essay fulfills the following requirements:

- It is a complete sentence.
- It is limited to one clear idea.
- It expresses an attitude or an opinion.
- It is a statement that can be argued.

A. Read each item. Write *yes* if it is an arguable thesis statement for an essay. Write *no* if it is not.

1. _____ A child's first five years.

2. _____ Attending school is a privilege that we should not take for granted.

3. _____ A diet that is low in carbohydrates is the best way to maintain a healthy weight.

4. _____ Los Angeles and New York are about 3,000 miles apart.

5. _____ I would like to discuss the air conditioning system in our school.

6. _____ High ticket prices and athletes that are paid too much.

7. _____ The 2002 Olympic Games were held in Salt Lake City in the United States.

8. _____ Changing your bedspread will give a new feel to your room, but don't forget to hang new curtains, too.

9. _____ Francis Scott Key wrote "The Star-Spangled Banner" in 1814.

Reread each item you thought was *not* a good thesis statement. Then write an improved version of each item on the lines below.

_____

_____

_____

_____

_____

_____

B. Write a good thesis statement based on
each of these topics.

1. *traveling*

_____

_____

2. *cell phones*

_____

_____

3. *twins*

_____

4. *big-city life*

_____

5. *vacations*

_____

6. *after-school jobs*

_____

7. *the use of makeup*

_____

8. *dressing in style*

_____

9. *wearing uniforms to school*

_____

10. *being an only child*

_____

11. *music*

_____

Lesson 17

Writing a Letter to Request Information

In a letter requesting information, you should get right to the point. Reveal the information you want and ask any questions you have. Follow the same format that you would use for any business letter:

- Include your address so the reader can send a reply.
- Include the address of the person to whom you are writing.
- Use a formal greeting followed by a colon.
- Keep the body of the letter brief, clear, and polite.
- Use a polite closing followed by a comma.
- Thank the person for his or her assistance.
- Include your signature above your typed or printed name.

Here is a letter requesting information from the editor of *Aquarium* magazine. Notice that the writer gets directly to the point, presenting her questions simply and clearly.

859 Oak Avenue
Lexington, KY 40511
June 18, 2005

Editor, *Aquarium* Magazine
P.O. Box 83224
Campbell, CA 95008

Dear Sir or Madam:

I'm writing to ask about clownfish. I've always liked them, but I've never had one in my saltwater aquarium. I'm planning to get two or more of these fish, and I'd like you to answer a few questions. Is a five-gallon tank large enough for clownfish, or do I need a larger tank? Can I keep clownfish in the same tank with seahorses? What kind of food should I get for clownfish?

Thank you for your help.

Very truly yours,

Janice Owen

Janice Owen

Write a letter that requests information. You may choose one of the topics listed below, or use any other topic that interests you. Follow the format in the example on page 48.

Possible topics:

astronomy	ballet	calisthenics
dogs	ecology	gasoline
health	iguanas	lobsters
music	navigation	origami
perfumes	quilting	soccer
tennis	umbrellas	vitamins
wolves	X-rays	zebras

Lesson 18 — More Letter Writing

The letter you wrote in Lesson 17 was a business letter. Not all letters follow the same format. In a friendly letter, you don't need to include the address of the person to whom you are writing. The greeting has a friendlier tone and is followed by a comma. The closing is also friendlier than in a business letter. Notice the conversational format and tone of the example letter on the right.

683 Antelope Road
Camden, NJ 08101
June 15, 2004

Dear Cameron,

Congratulations on your graduation from high school! Uncle John and I are so proud of you.

I wish we could have been there to see the ceremony, but, as you know, John has been quite ill. He sends his love.

We're both looking forward to your visit this summer. Maybe we can play a few duets on the piano.

Affectionately,

Aunt Carolyn

A. In the space below, write a friendly letter of congratulations to a friend or relative. Follow the format used in the example.

A letter of congratulation, introduction, thanks, or support doesn't *always* have to be formatted as a friendly letter. Consider your audience before you decide whether to use a business format or a friendly format. If you're writing to a business associate, use a business format. For friends and family, use a friendly format.

B. Write the format you would use in each of the situations described below.

1. _____ Your cousin just got engaged to be married. You're writing to congratulate him.

2. _____ A member of your staff is moving. She has asked you to write her a letter of recommendation.

3. _____ You have just been interviewed for a job. You want to write a thank-you letter to the interviewer.

4. _____ Your grandparents sent you a check for your birthday. You want to write a note to thank them.

C. Now, choose one of the letter-writing situations above, or make up a real-life situation of your own that requires a letter. Write that letter in the space below. Be sure to use the format that is appropriate to the audience.

Nouns

Proper nouns, which name specific persons, places, or things, must be capitalized.
Common nouns are not capitalized. The number of the noun (singular or plural) used
as a subject determines the number of the verb used with it. It also determines the
number of any pronoun that refers to it. Here are some examples:

- **PROPER NOUNS:** Abigail, California, Brooklyn Bridge
- **COMMON NOUNS:** woman, state, bridge
- *SINGULAR NOUN* **WITH** <u>SINGULAR VERB</u>**:** *Abigail* <u>wants</u> to visit New York soon.
- *PLURAL NOUN* **WITH** <u>PLURAL VERB</u>**:** The two *friends* <u>want</u> to visit New York soon.
- *SINGULAR NOUN (ANTECEDENT)* **WITH** <u>SINGULAR PRONOUN</u>**:** *Jane* lost <u>her</u> umbrella.
- *PLURAL NOUN (ANTECEDENT)* **WITH** <u>PLURAL PRONOUN</u>**:** The *boys* bought <u>their</u> own tickets.

A. Write nouns or simple sentences as described below.

1. a. proper noun naming a relative: _____

    b. common noun naming a relative: _____

2. a. proper noun naming a city: _____

    b. common noun naming a place: _____

3. a. proper noun naming a building: _____

    b. common noun naming a building: _____

4. sentence using *apple* as the subject: _____

    _____

5. sentence using *grandparents* as the subject: _____

    _____

6. sentence using *Linda* as the subject: _____

    _____

7. sentence using *the Andersons* as the subject: _____

    _____

8. sentence using *computers* as the subject: _____

    _____

9. sentence using *Gary* as an antecedent for *his*: _____

    _____

B. Each of the following sentences has an error in capitalization or number. Circle the capitalization error or the noun that is used incorrectly. Then, rewrite the sentence correctly by changing the noun or adding or deleting capital letters.

1. The book were delivered to the store two weeks late.

    _____

2. The man need several new bookcases.

    _____

3. The Wilkinsons buys all her books online.

    _____

4. Wanda bought a travel book about austin, Texas.

    _____

5. Our city has about 10 Bookstores.

    _____

6. David will turn in her book report in May.

    _____

7. Maria passed his driving test the first time he took it.

    _____

8. Sixteen book were displayed on the shelf.

    _____

9. I bought this book in the gift store of the empire state building.

    _____

10. The vendors sold her entire stock of travel books.

    _____

11. This book is called *Master and commander*.

    _____

12. Diane gave more than a hundred Books to charity.

    _____

13. Mary's lifelong Love of books began in early childhood.

    _____

14. Her Grandmother read to her at every opportunity.

    _____

Lesson
19   Newspaper Story

When you scan the pages of a newspaper, you read the headlines first. A headline is like a title—but it is actually more than that. It has key words that tell what the article is about. When you see an interesting headline, you expect that the story will fill in the details. The story will usually answer the following questions: Who? What? When? Where? Why?

A. Read this example of a news story. Then, answer the questions that follow.

EXPLOSION DESTROYS FACTORY

June 13—A San Pedro sardine cannery and fireworks factory exploded at 2:45 last night. The building, shared by Tight Squeeze Sardines and Big Bad Blasters, was totally demolished by the blast. Two night security guards escaped without injury. No other workers were inside the building at the time.

Located at 4873 Gaffey Street, the old wooden building caught on fire at approximately 2:30 A.M. Heat from the fire caused the fireworks-making supplies to explode and blast the roof off the building. As sardines rained down on the surrounding buildings, firefighters fought to control the fire. The blaze was under control by 4:00 this morning.

Fire officials do not know the cause of the fire at this time.

"I'm glad we managed to get out before the explosion," said security guard Darwin Winters. "The blast sounded like a bomb going off. We're both lucky to be alive."

1. What is the story about? _____

2. Where did the disaster happen? _____

3. Who was involved? _____

4. When did it happen? _____

5. Why did it happen? _____

_____

B. Write your own news story, answering the five Ws of journalism. You may base your story on any of the following ideas, or use one of your own.

a football game   state budget problems   a big storm

a car accident   a political election campaign   a medical breakthrough

a senate vote   a meeting between heads of state   a chemical spill

a new law   a city planning meeting   a train wreck

Lesson 20   Problem-and-Solution Essay

What would you do if your dog misbehaved or your cat clawed the furniture? What if you wanted to decorate a room but had only $75.00 to spend? What if you were having great trouble understanding the material in a textbook? Or perhaps your kitchen is overrun with ants! Whatever the problem, there is probably a solution—if only you are creative enough to see it!

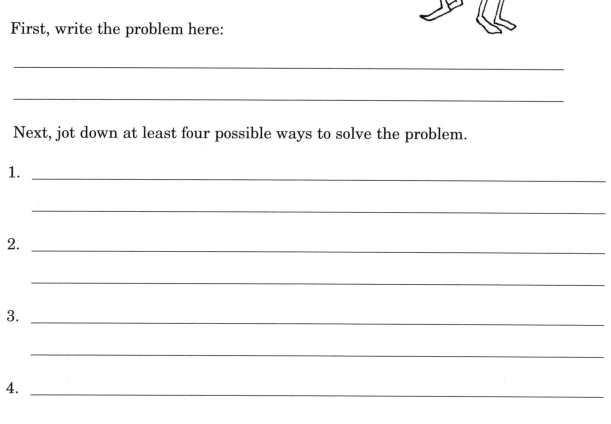

A. Outline a problem-and-solution essay about a problem you have now or have had in the past. Follow these pointers as you write:

- Begin with a description of the problem.

- Speculate about the cause of the problem.

- Make several suggestions about how to solve the problem.

- Indicate which suggestion you think would be the most effective.

- Comment on the anticipated outcome.

First, write the problem here:

_____

_____

Next, jot down at least four possible ways to solve the problem.

1. _____

    _____

2. _____

    _____

3. _____

    _____

4. _____

    _____

B. Using the notes you made on page 56, write a problem-and-solution essay here. As you write, pay special attention to effective sentence order. You might want to begin with the best solution, or you might want to lead up to the best solution. (Hint: It would *not* be a good idea to bury the best suggestion in the middle!)

Lesson 21

School Report: An Admirable Person

All of us admire other people for various reasons. We may think they're especially attractive, virtuous, effective, important, charitable, or accomplished. We may see them as very athletic, dedicated, generous, talented, or stylish.

A. Think about the people you admire. They can be from the past or the present. Make a list here:

_____   _____

_____   _____

_____   _____

Now, choose two of the people on your list. Complete one of the cluster diagrams below for each person by listing the reasons each person deserves admiration. Write the person's name in the center circle. Write your reasons in the outer circles.

1.

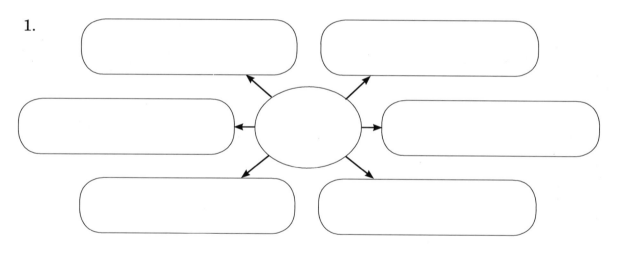

2.

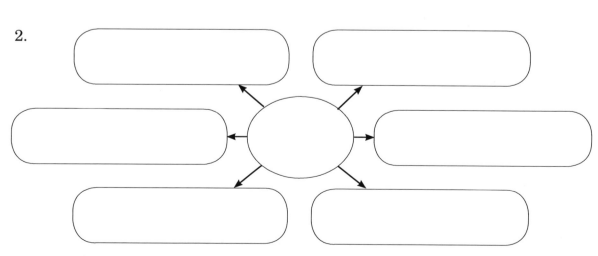

—

B. Now, choose one of the names from your cluster diagrams. Write a first draft of a brief essay explaining why that person deserves admiration. Use the details in your diagram as the basis of your essay. As you write, follow these tips:

- Use examples effectively.
- Vary your sentence length.
- Differentiate between fact and opinion.

- Use reference resources, including the Internet, effectively.
- Use effective sentence order, making your strongest points either first or last—but not buried in the middle!

Now, revise your first draft, making a clean copy of your final, corrected essay.

The Writing Process:
Paraphrasing and Summarizing

Paraphrasing and summarizing—what's the difference between the two?
Read these definitions:

> **Paraphrasing** is the act of restating an author's idea in different words.
> The purpose of paraphrasing is to clarify the author's meaning for the reader.
>
> **Summarizing** is the act of briefly stating the main ideas and supporting
> details presented in a longer piece of writing.

Here is an example of an author's original words followed by a paraphrase:

*"Down the mountain, moving beyond a curtain of quivering air, she saw the stage
coming, perhaps with letters."* (Wallace Stegner, *Angle of Repose*)

paraphrase: She saw the stage coming from below, possibly carrying mail.

Here is the entire original paragraph and a summary of it:

*"Down the mountain, moving beyond a curtain of quivering air, she saw the stage
coming, perhaps with letters. If she started in five minutes, she would arrive at the
Cornish Camp post office at about the same time as the stage. But the post office
was in the company store, where there were always loiterers—teamsters, drifters,
men hunting work—whom Oliver did not want her to encounter alone. And Ewing,
the manager of the store, was a man she thought insolent. She must wait another
two hours, till Oliver came home, to know whether there was mail. If the truth were
known, these days she always looked at his hands, for the gleam of paper, before
she looked at his face."*

summary: She saw the stage coming, possibly with mail. She could go to the Cornish
Camp post office to find out, but she didn't like the men who loitered there. She'd have
to wait two hours for Oliver to come home. Then she could find out if there was any mail.

Following the examples above, write paraphrases or summaries for the
following quotations.

1. "He felt apprehension so strongly that at one point it seemed to tighten
   his throat and nearly caused him to choke on a bite of cornbread."
   (Larry McMurtry, *Lonesome Dove*)

   PARAPHRASE: _____

   _____

   _____

2. "I trust that the reader has been enabled, by the preceding chapters, to form some conception of the magnificence of the streets of Venice during the course of the thirteenth and fourteenth centuries." (John Ruskin, *The Stones of Venice*)

PARAPHRASE: _____

_____

_____

3. "There is no shortage of good days. It is good lives that are hard to come by. A life of good days lived in the senses is not enough. The life of sensation is the life of greed; it requires more and more. The life of the spirit requires less and less; time is ample and its passage sweet. Who would call a day spent reading a good day? But a life spent reading—that is a good life. A day that closely resembles every other day of the past ten or twenty years does not suggest itself as a good one. But who would not call Pasteur's life a good one, or Thomas Mann's?" (Annie Dillard, *The Writing Life*)

SUMMARY: _____

_____

_____

_____

_____

4. "As she grew older the group, the herd, which is any collection of children, began to sense what adults felt, that there was something foreign about Cathy. After a while only one person at a time associated with her. Groups of boys and girls avoided her as though she carried a nameless danger." (John Steinbeck, *East of Eden*)

SUMMARY: _____

_____

_____

_____

_____

Essay

Follow these steps to write an essay:

1. **Prewriting: Choose a Subject**

   Make a list of possible subjects for an essay. Your subjects can be based on history, current events, favorite authors, controversial issues, sports, science, or anything else that interests you.

   _____   _____

   _____   _____

   _____   _____

   Now narrow your list of possibilities by asking yourself questions like these: Why am I interested in this subject? Can I make it interesting for others? Will I be able to find enough facts to support my thesis? What resources will give me this information? Once you've answered these questions, write your final topic choice here:

   _____

2. **Prewriting: Narrowing the Subject**

   Make sure your subject is narrow enough to cover in an essay. Obviously, "the history of Egypt," "World War II," or "filmmaking" are too broad. You need to focus on just one aspect of the subject— one that can be thoroughly discussed in a short paper. Here is how one student narrowed down the topic of automobiles:

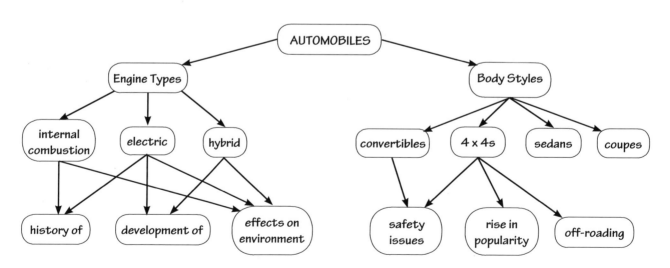

   A suitable subtopic for a short paper might be the environmental effects of the internal combustion engine.

Using the model, make a topic web for your own chosen subject.

Write your narrowed subject here: _____

3. Prewriting: Gathering Details

Before writing your first draft, you need to gather details for your essay. Use a variety of sources, such as books, periodicals, and the Internet. You might also want to interview someone who has special knowledge of the subject. Take notes on separate note cards, identifying the source of the information. You might need to cite the source in footnotes and a bibliography, so be sure to take accurate and legible notes.

4. Prewriting: Organizing Information

Now, organize your cards into sections of related information. As you read through your cards, look for one idea that can be supported by most of the information. This can be developed into your thesis statement, or main idea. Eliminate notes that do *not* support your main idea.

Write your thesis statement here:_____

_____

5. Drafting

After organizing your notes, begin a first draft of your paper. As you write, follow these tips:

- Refer to your notes and plan of organization.

- Stay aware of your audience and purpose.

- Get your ideas down on paper without worrying about every little detail of mechanics. You can polish your work later.

- Write a strong introduction that captures the readers' attention. State your thesis toward the end of the introduction.

- Write the body of the paper, supporting and developing your thesis with solid evidence. You can use facts, statistics, quotations from experts, and so on. Use footnotes to credit all words and ideas that are not your own.

- Write an effective conclusion. You might end with a strong quotation, a prediction, a recommendation to your audience, or a compelling question.

6. **Revising and Editing**

Revise your work, looking for places where you can improve it. Ask yourself questions like these:

- Is the thesis clearly stated?

- Can any unnecessary information be deleted?

- Does the style of the paper suit the audience?

- Is the paper well-organized?

- Within paragraphs in the body, are all topic sentences clear? Are they well-supported by details?

- Can transitional words and phrases be added to improve the flow of your writing?

- Have you credited sources for words and ideas that are not your own?

7. **Have a peer (fellow student) review your work.**

This is always a good idea. Why? Another pair of eyes might see something that you missed. Peers can help each other improve their work.

8. **Proofread your paper.**

Make sure of the spelling, grammar, and mechanics. Errors in these areas can be distracting to your audience.

9. **Make a final copy and publish it.**

You can publish your finished paper in many ways. Here are some ideas:

- Post a copy on a bulletin board in the classroom or on an electronic bulletin board.

- Present your paper orally.

- E-mail your paper to friends.

To the Teacher

"Practice is the best of all instructors." —Publilius Syrus, *Maxim*

Let's face it: *Most* students need to improve their writing skills.

All too often, student work is blemished by poorly composed sentences, misspelled words, and punctuation errors. The meaning the student writer intended to convey is unclear, if not downright confusing. What's the solution? The venerable old Roman got it right more than 2,000 years ago: practice, practice, and more practice!

Saddleback's WRITING 4 series links writing to purpose. Each of the four workbooks: NARRATIVE, EXPOSITORY, DESCRIPTIVE, and PERSUASIVE, specifically focuses on one particular "reason for writing." Each workbook contains 21 applications lessons and seven basic skills practice lessons. Relevant applications include drafting personal and business letters, narrating an historical event, and reviewing a movie. Specific skills taught include analyzing your audience, recognizing propaganda, creating tone, and sorting fact and opinion. Fundamental skills and concepts such as main idea, supporting details, and writing introductions and conclusions are reviewed in all four workbooks.

ONGOING ASSESSMENT

Periodic checks of student workbooks are highly recommended. If possible, assign peer tutors to coach remediation.

LESSON EXTENSIONS

To reinforce and enrich the workbook exercises, you may want to assign "extra credit" activities such as the following:

✓ write step-by-step instructions for some task that individual students know how to do, e.g., make a salad, repair a flat tire, etc.

✓ record the stories they write, or read them aloud to students in other classrooms

✓ write independent descriptions of the same event or object; then compare and contrast, discussing viewpoint, vocabulary, and level of detail

✓ bring in "letters to the editor" from newspapers and magazines to analyze and discuss in class

✓ write employment reference letters for each other

✓ critique TV commercials or ads they've seen in the print media

✓ write directions for walking or driving from one point to another, e.g., home to school, library to home, etc.

✓ interview a parent or a school employee, and then "write up" the interview for an article in the school newspaper

ANSWER KEY

LESSON 1: The Five Ws (pp. 6–7)

A. 1. all those interested in helping

2. decide on a theme for the dance and establish subcommittees for decorations, entertainment, chaperones, refreshments, and election of the king and queen and their court

3. Thursday, March 4, at 3:30 in the afternoon

4. every Thursday at the same time until the last week of May

5. in Room 314

6. to organize the prom

B. 1. Gertrude Ederle and Sebastian Tirabocchi

2. Ederle was the first woman to swim the English Channel.

3. August 6, 1926

4. between Cape Gris-Nez, France, and England

5. POSSIBLE ANSWER: I wanted to prove that women can compete in difficult and dangerous sports.

LESSON 2: Messages (pp. 8–9)

A. Missing information includes the caller's name and number.
POSSIBLE ANSWER FOR A BETTER MESSAGE:
Joan: Michael Timoney called about Friday night. He mentioned a dance. Call him back at 555-3348. If he's not home, call his cell at 555-3349.

B. POSSIBLE MESSAGE FOR JAKE:
Jake: Barry Watson called about your job application at the ice cream store on Birch Street. Call for an interview from noon to nine every day but Sunday. Phone number is 555-3972.

LESSON 3: Filling Out Forms (pp. 10–11)

A. Form should be filled out accurately.

B.

	TIME CARD				
Week of: _(last week's dates)_					
Employee: _(student's name)_					

DAY OF WEEK	TOTAL HOURS WORKED	REGULAR PAY	SICK PAY	VACATION PAY	OVERTIME
MON.	(holiday)	8 hrs			
TUES.	8 hrs	8 hrs			
WED.	10.5 hrs	8 hrs			2.5 hrs
THUR.	8 hrs	8 hrs			
FRI.	8 hrs	6.5 hrs	1.5 hrs		

BASIC SKILLS PRACTICE: Prewriting: Gathering Resource Information (pp. 12–13)

A. Answers will vary.

B. 1. encyclopedia 2. atlas 3. biography
4. Internet 5. Internet, magazines
6. personal interviews 7. biographies
8. biographies, documentaries

LESSON 4: Résumé and Cover Letter (pp. 14–15)

A. 1. Prepared 15 sandwiches per hour.

2. Filed correspondence for three attorneys.

3. Greeted clients, answered the phone, and made appointments.

4. Owned and operated a busy bike-repair shop for two years.

5. Closed the shop and secured the building at the end of each workday.

Each choice uses active verbs to describe specific duties and tells about the important work done in previous jobs.

B. Cover letter should be checked for accuracy.

LESSON 5: Office Memo, E-Mail (pp. 16–17)

A. POSSIBLE ANSWERS:
OUTLINE: TOPIC SENTENCE: mention being new manager; talk about future success of Tony's SUPPORTING SENTENCES: ask for employees' help; mention being open to all new ideas; give info about where and when to talk to me CLOSING SENTENCE: mention teamwork

MEMO:

Date: (current date)

To: All Employees

From: (student's name)

Regarding: Management Policy

Message: As the new manager of Tony's Sandwich Shop, my goal is to make Tony's even more successful than it is now. I cannot do this alone—I need the help of all employees. I am open to all new ideas for making Tony's more efficient. Please bring your ideas to me before or after your shifts. If you wish, you can call me at home between 5:00 and 7:00 in the evening. My home number is 555-2964. Together we can make Tony's a better place to work and a better place for our customers.

B. Sample e-mail:

Hi, Melanie,

Please send an arrangement of pink roses, white orchids, yellow daffodils, and purple irises to Tina Miller at the following address: 483 Trask Avenue, Lincoln Park, MI 48146. The customer wants to spend no more than $90.00. Send an invoice to me, and I'll send you a check, minus my 20 percent commission.

LESSON 6: How-To Directions (pp. 18–19)

A. 1. Assemble these supplies on the counter: loaf of bread, sliced turkey, sliced cheese, lettuce leaves, sliced tomato, mayonnaise.

2. Remove two slices of bread from the package.

3. Place the bread slices side by side on a plate.

4. Put a thin layer of mayonnaise on each slice of bread.

5. Arrange turkey slices and cheese on one slice of bread.

6. Arrange lettuce and tomato on the other slice of bread.

7. Put the two halves of the sandwich together.

8. Slice sandwich in halves or quarters.

B. Check students' own how-to directions for accuracy.

BASIC SKILLS PRACTICE: Sentences: Adding Details (pp. 20–21)

A. and B. Check students' work for interesting details.

LESSON 7: First-Aid Instructions (pp. 22–23)

Check students' first-aid instructions for format (bulleted, numbered, or lettered list) and accuracy, based on the sample paragraph.

LESSON 8: Transportation Directions (pp. 24–25)

B. SAMPLE ANSWER:

Go south on Fountain Square Drive to Greenback Lane.

Turn right and go to Van Maren Lane.

Turn right again, and go to the end of the road, turning left when Van Maren becomes Navion.

Take Navion southwest until it becomes Sunmist Way, which takes you to the cemetery.

C. Check students' directions against the map.

LESSON 9: Product Warning Label (pp. 26–27)

A., B., and C. Answers will vary.

BASIC SKILLS PRACTICE: Grammar: Pronoun-Antecedent Agreement (pp. 28–29)

A. 2. from *her* to *woman:* correct

3. from *he* to *woman:* A large crowd gathered around the woman as <u>she</u> painted.

4. from *she* to *Ms. Stevens:* correct

5. from *it* to *paintings:* She chooses paintings she likes and makes copies of <u>them</u>.

6. from *your* to *artists:* Artists who copy the masters improve <u>their</u> own techniques.

7. from *it* to *copies:* Many artists have made copies of great masterpieces, selling <u>them</u> to clients.

8. from *they* to *everyone:* correct

9. from *it* to *paintings:* Sally copies great paintings because she cannot afford to buy <u>them</u>.

10. from *they* to *copy:* To prevent forgeries, a copy cannot be the same size as the original <u>it</u> represents.

B. Since the day <u>it</u> opened in November 1793, the Louvre has allowed artists to copy the masterpieces it owns. In fact, it encourages <u>them</u> to come in and paint copies. French citizens fill out a simple form stating the date <u>they</u> <u>wish</u> to begin and the <u>paintings</u> <u>they</u> <u>wish</u> to copy. Non-French artists must also attach <u>copies</u> of <u>their</u> <u>passports</u> and <u>recommendations</u> from <u>their</u> <u>embassies</u>. The Louvre has an official stamp that <u>it</u> affixes to both sides of each copy. Copies of masterpieces must be one-fifth smaller or larger than originals, and <u>they</u> must also be inspected before leaving the museum.

LESSON 10: Product Labels (pp. 30–31)

Answers will vary.

LESSON 11: Writing to Compare and Contrast (pp. 32–33)

A. and B. Answers will vary. Check students' explanations and sentences for accuracy.

LESSON 12: Announcements and Invitations (pp. 34–35)

A. and B. Answers will vary. Check students' announcements, invitations, and obituaries.

BASIC SKILLS PRACTICE: Mechanics: Proofreading (pp. 36–37)

1. The Vaganova ballet academy is a dance school in St. Petersburg.

   The Vaganova Ballet Academy is a dance school in St. Petersburg.

2. This russian ballet school was founded in 1738

   This Russian ballet school was founded in 1738.

3. The school is is named after Agrippini vaganova, one of its Teachers.

   The school is named after Agrippini Vaganova, one of its teachers.

4. Potential students have must a medical examination before enrolling.

   Potential students must have a medical examination before enrolling.

5. Classes and practice each day, six days a weak, for eight years.

   POSSIBLE ANSWER: Classes and practice are required each day, six days a week, for eight years.

6. For every student admitted, nine are turned away about 60 are admitted each year.

   For every student admitted, nine are turned away. About 60 are admitted each year.

7. For practice, students may ware tights, leotards and shorts.

   For practice, students may wear tights, leotards, and shorts.

8. Wouldnt you like to join american ballet company? Emma asked. I'd prefer to study someplace in europe Mikhail replied.

   "Wouldn't you like to join an American ballet company?" Emma asked.
   "I'd prefer to study someplace in Europe," Mikhail replied.

LESSON 13: Planning for an Interview (pp. 38–39)

A. and B. Answers will vary.

LESSON 14: Taking Notes (pp. 40–41)

A. 1. Notes can help Myra find her way to the library. The notes should include street names, the directions (left, right, south, north, east, west) she should turn at various points, and the street address of the library.

2. Notes can help Jon's father get the correct message. Jon's notes should include the name and number of the caller, along with a brief message.

3. Notes can help David remember what he learns in his research. His notes should include the name of the store and information about the different brands, features, prices, and options of the computers he researches.

4. Notes will help Alicia make her connections. Her notes should include bus schedules and the locations of bus stops.

5. Notes will help Jerome remember where and when the skateboarding contest is. He should include the address, date, and time of the contest.

6. Notes will help Pat remember important details. He should take notes that answer the five Ws about the Vietnam War.

B. Paragraphs about the koala will vary. Check students' work for accuracy, based on the notes.

LESSON 15: Short-Answer Test Questions (pp. 42–43)

All the sample answers have superfluous information. Revised answers:

1. Forces deep within the earth continually affect the earth's surface. The energy from these forces is stored within the rocks. When this energy is released suddenly, an earthquake occurs.

2. Ponce de León came from Spain and explored Florida in 1513. Another famous explorer was Hernando Cortés, a Spanish adventurer who conquered Mexico in 1519–1521.

3. A jury that is unable to reach a verdict of guilty or not guilty is called a "hung jury." When this happens, the result is a mistrial.

4. The Mesozoic Era is more popularly known as the Age of Reptiles. This era began 245 million years ago and lasted for 180 million years.

5. The Taj Mahal is a marble mausoleum in India. It was built in the seventeenth century by a king for his wife.

BASIC SKILLS PRACTICE: Vocabulary: Precise Word Choice (pp. 44–45)

A. and B. Answers will vary.

LESSON 16: Thesis Statements for Essay Questions (pp. 46–47)

A. 1. no 2. yes 3. yes 4. no 5. no
6. no 7. no 8. no 9. no

Students' improved thesis statements and new thesis statements will vary.

POSSIBLE ANSWERS:

1. A child's first five years can mean the difference between a successful life and an unsuccessful life.

4. New York is a far more exciting city than Los Angeles.

5. The antiquated air conditioning system in our school has contributed directly to the poor health of some of our students.

6. The salaries of baseball players should be adjusted downward so that ticket prices could be lowered.

7. Downhill racing is the most exciting sport in the Olympic Games.

8. Changing your bedspread will give a new feel to your room.

9. "The Star-Spangled Banner" may not be the best choice for our national anthem.

B. POSSIBLE ANSWERS:

1. Traveling is a waste of money.

2. We'd all be better off without cell phones.

3. Life is harder for twins because they always have to share their parents' attention.

4. Big-city life offers greater opportunities for young people to learn about culture than small-town life does.

5. Workers in America need more vacation time.

6. After-school jobs invariably affect students' grades negatively.

7. Girls younger than 16 should not be allowed to use makeup.

8. It's more important to dress in the current style than to dress in becoming clothes.

9. A person who has to wear a uniform to school can never develop a sense of style.

10. Being an only child is a great advantage when it comes to having money for college.

11. To accompany the evening meal, classical music is the best choice.

LESSON 17: Writing a Letter to Request Information (pp. 48–49)

Answers will vary. Check students' letters for correct style and format.

LESSON 18: More Letter Writing (pp. 50–51)

A. Check students' letters for style and format.

B. 1. friendly   3. business
2. business   4. friendly

C. Check students' letters for style and format.

BASIC SKILLS PRACTICE: Nouns (pp. 52–53)

A. Sample answers:
1. a. Aunt Katherine
   b. uncle
2. a. Albuquerque
   b. mall
3. a. Transamerica Building
   b. library
4. The apple has a worm in it.
5. Darla's grandparents sent her a check for her birthday.
6. Linda threw a spectacular party for her daughter's graduation.
7. The Andersons spent their summer vacation at Lake Tahoe.
8. Ten new computers were delivered to the school.
9. Gary lent his car to Geraldine.

B. 1. book; The books were delivered to the store two weeks late.
2. man; The men need several new bookcases.
3. The Wilkinsons; Miss Wilkinson buys all her books online.
4. austin; Wanda bought a travel book about Austin, Texas.
5. Bookstores; Our city has about 10 bookstores.

6. David; Diane (or any girl's name) will turn in her book report in May.

7. Maria; Mario (or any boy's name) passed his driving test the first time he took it.

8. book; Sixteen books were displayed on the shelf.

9. empire state building; I bought this book in the gift store of the Empire State Building.

10. vendors; The vendor sold her entire stock of travel books.

11. commander; This book is called *Master and Commander*.

12. Books; Diane gave more than a hundred books to charity.

13. Love; Mary's lifelong love of books began in early childhood.

14. Grandmother; Her grandmother read to her at every opportunity.

LESSON 19: Newspaper Story (pp. 54–55)

A. 1. an explosion

2. in a building shared by a sardine cannery and a fireworks factory

3. two security guards

4. at 2:45 on the night of June 13

5. A fire caused the fireworks supplies to explode, but no one knows what caused the fire.

B. Students' stories will vary. Check for answers to the five Ws.

LESSON 20: Problem-and-Solution Essay (pp. 56–57)

A. and B. Answers will vary.

LESSON 21: School Report: An Admirable Person (pp. 58–59)

A. and B. Answers will vary.

BASIC SKILLS PRACTICE: The Writing Process: Paraphrasing and Summarizing (pp. 60–61)

POSSIBLE ANSWERS:

1. His strong sense of fear made his throat tighten to the point that he almost choked on some cornbread.

2. I hope that the reader has been able to visualize and understand the beauty of Venice streets during the 1400s and the 1500s.

3. Good days are easy to come by, but good lives are something else. A good life includes a spiritual side and is the opposite of a sensational life.

4. As Cathy got older, other children began to see her as different and so began avoiding her.

FINAL PROJECT: Essay (pp. 62–64)

Students' essays will vary.